Building Resilience

After Adverse Childhood Experiences (ACEs)

Rafe Nauen

Copyright © 2019
Rafe L Nauen

Printed in the United States of America and Europe

First Printing, 2019

ISBN 978 1080907038

Rafe Nauen
3 Mayfield Road
DERBY
DE21 6FX
UK
http://building-resilience.co.uk
http://books.rafenauen.com
rafe@rafenauen.com
+447889 523164

Contents

Dedication

Billy – my beloved cat who died when I was 15 and who provided a key to my resilience throughout my life. Now in my late 60's I am beginning to realise the significance of Billy, and recognise that attending to that, even now, helped me through what could have been a very dark period in my life. His affection and care were the start of a highly resilient life. He was the same age as me when we got him – I was 6 months old. He died when I was 15 and he got a state funeral – union flag draped over an orange box and I played the last post on the bugle.

Acknowledgements

Family – my family of origin, and the three systems of family that I have been part of during my life thus far, plus my Thursday group (a group of profoundly enlightened people who have helped me more than they will ever know) – Lou Radford, Andrea Spencer, Sarah Hobby and my extraordinary wife Julie Bowman who works with Limbic Reflexology and Flower Essences, Nadine Burke Harris, Isaac Pizer, Richard Wallstein. The clients who have taught me so much and have made this book both needed and possible.

Introduction

This is a follow-on book from Adverse Childhood Experiences: Using Constellation Therapy to help repair the damage

It has been shown many times that the outcomes from high ACEs scores are reduced significantly by the ability to gain resilience and this book is designed to aid you in a) finding the things that will help, and be b) noticing and upgrading the things that were already there.

Very recently a policeman told of being called to a domestic violence incident. A young lad who was probably very scared, sat in the policeman's car and the policeman turned on a mindfulness app on his phone, closed his eyes and told the lad to do the same. In that moment, the lad was trusted, seen, heard and respected – and many would underestimate the significance of that single moment in resilience terms. In my experience, those moments are massive.

In the dedication, I mention Billy, my cat. An ordinary ginger tom cat. BUT on three separate occasions he walked half a mile across a park and crossed a busy main road to meet me at the bus stop after difficult days at school. No-one had shown him where the bus stop was. But in those three occasions, he showed me that I had been seen and heard. It was the early days of life where my self-assurance and resilience met with the difficulties of normal existence and without that resilience could have sent me downhill.

What is Resilience?

Literally the capacity to recover quickly from difficulties or in other words, toughness.

Scenario: You're in the woods, and a bear suddenly appears before you. Several things happen.

1. The amygdala kicks in (that's the old primitive part of the brain)
2. cortisol (stress hormone) is secreted.
3. Adrenaline is released
4. The heart rate goes up
5. Breathing goes heavier and deeper
6. The temperature of the body goes up
7. The rational brain (modern brain) shuts down

This is all so that a very fast (and not necessarily rational) decision gets made to either run like hell or fight and kill the bear.

That's all good when it is a bear in the woods. When it's an unpredictable alcoholic mother that is triggering the adrenals then persistent hypervigilance will threaten physical and mental health for the whole of life. Resilience is the ability to return to calm and rational thought quickly. A child that lives in a violent household but has an adult neighbour who listens and is able to reduce the tension and make a safe space available will enable that child to build resilience so that adversity is seen as something that happens and can be dealt with. They will learn to bounce!

Source: https://psychcentral.com/lib/what-is-resilience/

By Harold Cohen, Ph.D.
Last updated: 8 Oct 2018

When faced with adversity in life, how does a person cope or adapt? Why do some people seem to bounce back from tragic events or loss much more quickly than others? Why do some people seem to get "stuck" in a point in their life, without the ability to move forward?

Psychologists have long studied these issues and have come up with a label you may be familiar with **resilience.** When faced with a tragedy, natural disaster, health concern, relationship, work, or school problem, resilience is how well a person can adapt to the events in their life. A person with good resilience can bounce back more quickly and with less stress than someone whose resilience is less developed.

Everybody has resilience. It's just a question of how much and how well you put it to good use in your life. Resilience doesn't mean the person doesn't feel the intensity of the event or problem. Instead, it just means that they've found a pretty good way of dealing with it more quickly than others.

Everyone can learn to increase their resilience abilities. Like any human skill, learning greater resilience is something that you can do at any age, from any background, no matter your education or family relationships. All you need to do in order to increase your resilience is have the willingness to do so. And then seek out ways of learning more about resilience, with the help of a trained therapist. Changing outcomes is the realm of epigenetics

Genetics are what is handed down from parent to child in their DNA. Epigenetics is the modification of gene expression, rather than alteration of the gene itself. (EPI is a Greek prefix that means "on top of"). So, it it's like having a pile of Lego bricks – you can make many different models with the same bricks – some will be stronger than others and utilise the bricks in a different way.

Building Resilience is the art of using the bricks you happen to have to the best of any one's ability.

Resilience for some and not for others?

So why do some kids get resilience in spades, and others seem to manage badly. The answer is the brain system is twofold – on the one hand the amygdala is function well to get you to chose fight or flight or freeze (see later in the book) but also the system needs some dopamine – the pleasure function, and that will be down to availability. If the dopamine comes from ready access to love and hugs from a devoted mummy (or in my case a cat) then that will do. But if there is nothing around then drink or drugs will also perform that function, even though the net result may be a downward spiral.

So when you are reviewing your journey, just check on the availability and that's where you will find a curious neighbour that *saw* you, or maybe a teacher that was interested in a quirky hobby. It all builds resilience

Resilience versus Compliance

Compliance is performing according solely to the agenda of others. A compliant person will do what they have been told to do, despite their own judgements, and consequently may feel constantly wrong footed when things don't work out as was planned.

By and large, most parents wish their children to develop into completely independent human adults. It's also true that having a highly independent 2-year-old is somewhat of a handful. The balance is all about timing – when does independence become okay within a family setup. Most people would wish their two-year-old child to be compliant and simply do as they are told along the lines of "mummy knows best …" If the child does not tackle independence during his or her growing up years then they may never discover who they really are, and what makes them tick – they may become classic "people pleasers" – people who respond to others requirements for their action and non-action.

Personally, I have seldom compromised my soul for another, and that statement may seem egoistical, but is reality, self-preservation. The classic is on a plane, the stewards will always tell you to put on your own oxygen mask BEFORE you attend to others, because if you're not breathing you certainly cannot help others. My brother Richard was compliant – and seldom in trouble with my parents. I was resilient and often in trouble. But in later life, my brother really wasn't sure who he was even. He had been a successful lawyer in Sheffield since graduating but confessed that he had never enjoyed it. My parents suggested he would be a lawyer when he was four because he was argumentative. He retired to Fuertaventura in his 50's but took his own life in 2004 aged 57. It had always appeared that his childhood was easier than mine, but in truth he had to compromise his own being persistently to ingratiate himself with my parents. I didn't. It was genuinely what he believed he was supposed to do, and so did I – but I just couldn't – that's resilience! I am also certain that coming out of a war and having children produced some controversial ideas about what one is supposed to do with three children.

My mother was fire warden in the second world war – so occasionally kicked firebombs off rooves, and periodically ushered people from their burning houses – a real hero. My father was a Royal Engineer soldier (sappers and miners) in Burma and saw horrific things he never spoke of when he returned. But the climate on his return was all about the ones that came back, and little was spoken of the heroes that stayed and served the civilian population whilst the war had raged. Their jobs were forgotten, and my mother would have had to hide all her stories to respect the inability of people like my father from speaking of the horrors they had witnessed. So, as an adult she used her compliance to become resilient – stiff upper lip.

I have a son and a son in law who work on ambulances – one as a paramedic and the other as a driver. They will sometimes engage in what used to be called gallows humour – highly non politically correct, but it is a powerful tool for disengaging from some of the things that they need to be calm about witnessing which other people might find traumatising. That tension release engages with some brain changes and obscures the normal flight mechanism when faced with trauma or deep stress. It would clearly not be great for an ambulance man to run away when confronted with a fatal road traffic collision. That would be the amygdala's normal response, and forcing a different response – clearly ambulance personnel need logic, rationality, calm, normal heart rate, normal breathing, no outward display of blushing in order to carry out a task in a situation that they have quite deliberately entered voluntarily (well, under instruction). Thus their balance is upheld – they are using their own resilience ("this is what I have been taught", "This is precisely what we trained for", "I've seen it all before", etc etc) to enable compliance ("ambulance 123 – proceed to RTA at junction of ... - believe there may be a fatality") If their resilience is good, then they decompress later, have a bath when they get home, have supper, and resume their job next day. If the resilience is not so strong, they might need some help, counselling etc in order to manage. But if they are fully compliant, a classic people pleaser, they might take responsibility in the form of "if I had got there sooner, they might not have died", or some such construct. For those, it's not a stretch to judge that ambulance driving might not be for them! But this is just an example of how the balance of compliance and resilience works out in real life.

Positives out of Negatives

Sometimes life throws you a curved ball that only with hindsight can you possibly see as a magnificent moment. I was at St Dunstan's College (a day public school) in Catford South London. Nearby in 1966 was Mr Smith's gambling club run by Paddy McKiernan and frequented by shotgun Frankie Richardson amongst others. It was where a murder happened) The Richardson gangs main rivals were the Krays. St Dunstan's was a middle class relatively expensive school (I had a free place after my 11 plus). The year I left (1968) my old school became a drug empire of sorts – affluent children who had business acumen coupled with an area where plenty of kids wanted to buy. I left because I failed all my O' Levels – twice. I had passed maths in 1966 and passed Chemistry and English Language – twice in 1969 at a crammer in London. I never touched drugs, but clearly see that had I sailed through my O' levels, with my temperament and my desire for popularity, I probably would have been a dealer by age 17 and probably dead by 35. So, resilience comes in all forms – Simply not being there is a brilliant protection skill!

But it means I can say hand on heart that failing my O' levels were one of the things that saved my life. So, I urge the reader to study their life story and just allow yourself to notice the things that happened that may have engaged with a long term positive. Like missing a plane journey that ends in disaster, even if you failed to get your ticket refunded. Without the disaster, you would of course kick yourself for daftness or whatever adjective you care to place on it. With the disaster, a bit of you exclaims "YES" and punches the air. Same experience for you, massively different outcomes for you based on entirely external circumstances.

As you perform that exercise of rather than revising history (which most history books do) I urge you to revise the way you notice what the longer-term outcomes were. What you will find is that many occurrences that have promoted your life, with other outcomes that have nothing to do with you, might have been many times worse. Ironically I worked for Paddy McKiernan in the 1970's. He had had to disappear from the London and Manchester scenes having helped the police put several gang members in prison. He ran a club in Pwllheli near where I lived, and shortage of money pushed me to re-engage with being a cook – so I worked at the Cadwallader Jones for about six months. My friend Nic Mucci and I helped remove all the fixtures and fittings from his Mr Smith's club in Winsford on the day the demolition started – in order to maximise his profits, he had to be running the night before the demolition! Resilience!!

Love and loyalty

What is love, and how does it compare to loyalty.

People talk of unconditional love, but what do they mean, and does that mean that you continue to accept the unacceptable for the whole of your life?

This is why I brought up the subject of loyalty.

Loyalty is a product of society and survival. Salmon don't need any loyalty whatsoever. If you (theoretically perhaps) get a salmon egg, hatch it alone; bring it up alone in a jar, then a tank etc; and then finally release it on different side of the UK to the one where you found it, science will inform you that it may well find its way back to its own original spawning river in where, having mated on the journey, it will spawn again in the motherland.

No such journey for a human. A human will learn none of those things, because it will seek out role models – ideally his or her perfect mother and father. So, he or she will seek a partner that is a close match to that role model. As you read this you will become aware of someone you know (perhaps yourself, or partner) that has clearly married their mother (for example) and it applies to both sexes and includes LBGT relationships too – the gender of the partner may not be included in the role model representation – that's loyalty for you.

In the case of absent parent or parents, other loyalties pertain. The son of a couple where the father has left early will often display attitudes and tastes that mirror the absent parent – deep down the loyalty to that parent enables a projection of loyalty. I use the example of a son and absent father because that is the most common example, certainly in my experience. The irony is that that mirroring may itself cause issues with the (staying) mother. And the girlfriends may well represent a repeat of that history, with some adjustments.

So, where does love fit into this equation? Well when the newly formed adult out of the relationship finds a match, the endorphins kick in and he or she reflects that back, and the bonding cycle begins. If it lasts a while it will be called love, and the deals will begin. Perhaps the couple want children themselves, so agree that as the mother becomes unavailable, the father will stay and support until such time as he is needed (taking kids out into the world etc etc). This seems like a very old world view, but the roles of mothering and fathering in early childhood are pretty much along those lines – the fathering does not have to be carried out by a man, nor does the mothering roles necessitate that main care giver to be a woman. And those deals and agreements are what we might term love in a family setting. Obviously, the word love is very inadequate for all the work it needs to do in the English language. It is said that Inuit people have hundreds of words for snow, but none for "please". We say:

1. I love my wife
2. I love my son
3. I love my cat
4. I love my house
5. I love that view
6. I love walks in the park
7. I love Eric Clapton

Clearly the good English speaker may well understand the different nuances I am managing and will interpret an understanding that correlates with what I wish to convey, but someone who has cursory understanding of English might be confused. In French there is the verb "Amour" which means love, as in the last 6 of my list, but "Adorer" which is the verb to love with all one's heart – hopefully representing the first!

So just across the channel from UK we have already found that love doesn't quite work as we wish to represent (especially on paper) the different categories of love.

So, to recap;

1 – adore, contract of agreement about love, and commitment

2,3 similar, but no endorphins! Definitely commitment – more for 2 than 3

4 commitment, no endorphins, and the agreement is not mutual – the house has not agreed to do anything for me – if the roof is damaged it will be me that repairs it

5,6&7 represent enjoyment and a sense of wellbeing but there is no mutuality – Eric Clapton does not know who I am (well I assume he doesn't)

1. Big mutual loyalty
2. Long term loyalty
3. Medium term loyalty (unlikely to outlive me)
4. One-way loyalty
5. No loyalty
6. No loyalty
7. No loyalty

FYI Endorphins are a group of hormones secreted by the pituitary gland which reduce pain and boost the sense of pleasure. Someone who genuinely feels happy a lot will have endorphins being released a lot too.

So, what's the purpose of this loyalty and the associated love model? It's to bind systems together – that sense of belonging is essential for the propagation of the species.

So, there are mechanisms in the brain that keep us addicted to love and loyalty. Unfortunately, the love aspect can, as discussed here, represent a number of different aspects, some of which might be far away from what the textbooks might call love – people in abusive relationships often stay far beyond that which logic would dictate. And for the child with high ACEs the implicit safety of the home might also represent the fear of attack, and hence the child will grow up with hyper vigilance surrounding him or her, and the concept of any kind of safe space could get lost. The same child in an environment where there is a safe space nearby – a neighbour who understands, and accepts the story as fact, or perhaps an elderly relative means that the child can decompress and recover. That resilience makes everything different because it prevents the brain from accepting that it is all about the victim. In the former case the child's brain develops without that control, and therefore will have less resilience from earlier childhood.

Brain Function

This chapter is here to show and explain what is going on in the brain chemistry when we experience stress.

Resilience enables us to reduce the impact, to challenge triggers and to remain calm in a crisis.

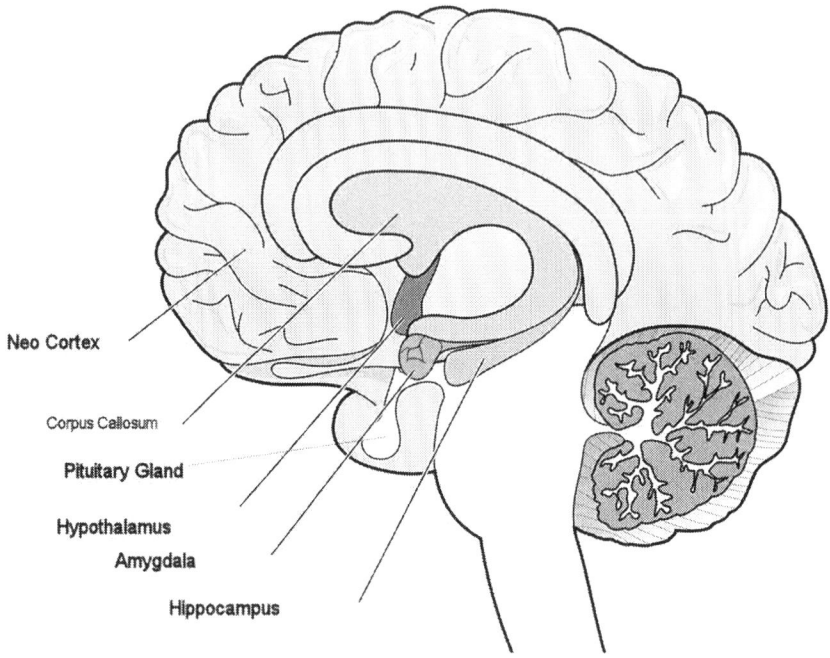

The older portions of the brain (the primordial stuff) is the amygdala, hypothalamus and hippocampus. These are used to prepare the primitive human for action when threatened – to keep you safe when danger is around. The later developments neo cortex and corpus callosum. The neo cortex is the rational part, the place of ethics, decisions, greater good concepts etc, and develop in the human later. Clearly a baby needs only to cry to get attention for food, health and love. It does not need reasoning skills until much later.

The two sides the brain control different aspects of humanity – the left being about logic, science maths, controls etc. The right side is about creativity and more artistic stuff – appreciation of beauty. The corpus callosum is a thick band of nerves that control the flow of information between the two hemispheres. In a study published in Science Daily it was shown that a significant proportion of psychopaths had an abnormal corpus callosum affecting the flow of information between the two sides of the hippocampus, thus removing feelings of guilt when perpetrating acts that non-psychopaths would be restrict from doing by their own systemic controls.

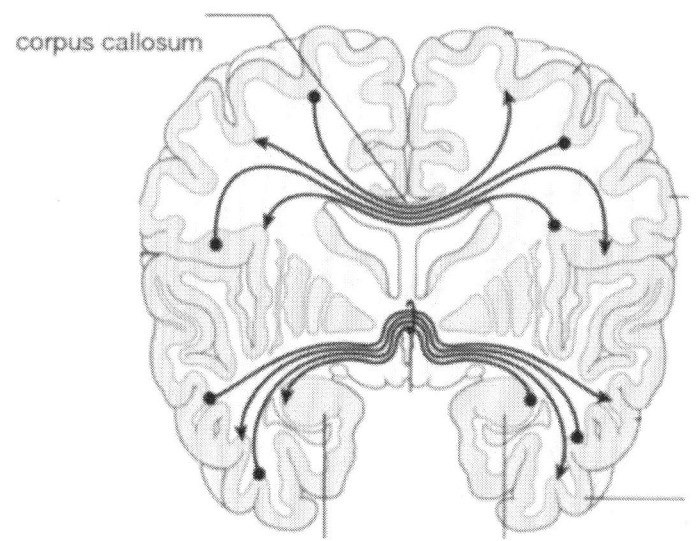

corpus callosum

Briefly:

Say you are in the woods, and you see a bear – several instant things happen:

1. The hypothalamus sends a signal to the pituitary gland saying "Urgent! Get the adrenals up and release stress hormones, adrenaline and cortisol, fast!!"
2. Your heart starts pounding, your pupils dilate, your airways open and your logical brain is put temporarily offline.
3. You're ready to fight anything or run faster than a rocket. You're ready – on high alert.

Picture the scenario where the bear in the woods is, you're unpredictable alcoholic mother. Adrenaline has kicked into action daily, and you become unable to differentiate real and perceived dangers. The result is that your brain becomes ready to react to the smell of lager (or whatever) and a pathway is opened in the neural structures.

What are ACEs

Adverse Childhood Experiences (ACEs) is the term used to describe all types of abuse, neglect, and other potentially traumatic experiences that occur to people under the age of 18.

Adverse Childhood Experiences have been linked to

risky health behaviours,

chronic health conditions,

low life potential, and

early death.

As the number of ACEs increases, so does the risk for these outcomes.

*Source CDC
https://www.cdc.gov/violenceprevention/childabuseandneglect/acestudy/aboutace.html

The score sheet in the Appendix section will display the sorts of issues that children (anyone under 18) might encounter that has been categorised as an ACE – and the scientific studies all point to the fact that the more ACEs, the higher the risk of life altering outcomes, and the thing that most astonished scientists dealing with the study results, is that the outcomes often relate to physical health in much later life, not just turbulent or poor mental health in earlier years.

Thus, dealing with the results of ACEs at ANY stage in life is crucial – it is literally never too late.

Clearly, bring children into a world where there are no ACEs available to them is one the best solutions, but if you find yourself with historic issues, you need to build on any resilience you already have. And if you are reading this book then you are trying to do something about that history.

In terms of when is too late, my answer is that the most elderly client I have had so far was 91 when she first came to see me, and she gained a lot of insight, and relaxed considerably. Some of her health issues were too late to tackle, but she felt better able to cope with them.

My youngest client was 3 – his daddy had left (definite ACE) but just listening to him and enabling him with PlayPeople™ to establish who everyone was in relation to him (including the new girlfriend), was enough to settle him and allow resilience to build.

A person with an ACE score of ten will have a harder time building the resilience needed to severely adjust their own life chances than a person with a score of night or one, but the project is still very much worthwhile.

And it should always be remembered that is much more likely for a person with a high ACEs score to be aware of the historic issues that prescribed some of the outcomes than a person who just felt unloved – it might take the latter person an age to realise that it

wasn't that they were unlovable.

What Therapies are useful?

Mindfulness

Mindfulness is the psychological process of bringing one's attention to experiences occurring in the present moment, which one can develop through the practice of meditation and through other training. Mindfulness is derived from sati, a significant element of Buddhist traditions and based on Zen and Tibetan meditation techniques. (Source Wikipedia).

Mindfulness techniques will allow the challenging of triggers so that the person recognises a trigger earlier on or even immediately it occurs and applies mindful challenges to the trigger. "I am being triggered by the smell of a school" "This school is clean and I am a teacher and therefore in authority in this school" "The trigger relates to experiences as a child, and no longer apply now" That dialogue might need to be even simpler or much more complex, but either way, you can see that the heat of the situation is taken out of the equation.

Emotional Freedom Techniques (EFT)

EFT is a form of counselling intervention that draws on various theories of alternative medicine including acupuncture, neuro-linguistic programming, energy medicine, and Thought Field Therapy (TFT). It is best known through Gary Craig's EFT Handbook, published in the late 1990s, and related books and workshops by a variety of teachers. EFT and similar techniques are often discussed under the umbrella term "energy psychology". (Source Wikipedia).

[23]

The use of EFT does give some control of state to the client – even young children, so that they can do something to alleviate feelings of danger, scaredness or other troublesome emotional states that they may experience from time to time.

The system draws on ancient research and practice in meridians in the body – as used in acupressure, and acupuncture, but rather using NLP type dialogue and at the same time triggering the meridians so that the neurotransmission of negative farming is interrupted and is replaced by positive framing. The technique uses several points on the body to focus. The big advantage is that once learned, the client can continue to use the technique at any time and in any circumstances, and one of the big issues with any trauma led issues is that triggers can range from very small, even apparently insignificant matters, even the smell of a school. Once triggered, the range of anguish experienced can be from negligible to catatonic.

Matrix Re-imprinting

Matrix uses EFT at its core, but then goes on to re-imprint over the original trauma version of a memory. EFT uses the meridians as does Matrix but with matrix there is an opportunity to freeze frame a memory at the time of the trauma and then broaden the understanding so that the trauma disappears, leaving the memory un-traumatic.

NLP

Neuro-linguistic programming (**NLP**) is an approach to communication, personal development,
and psychotherapy created by Richard Bandler and John Grinder in California, United States in the 1970s. NLP's creators

claim there is a connection between neurological processes (neuro-), language (linguistic) and behavioural patterns learned through experience (programming), and that these can be changed to achieve specific goals in life. Source Wikipedia

Thus, when change of neurology is required as in the case of someone who is hypervigilant due to early childhood trauma, NLP can help to reframe.

Timeline Therapy™

Time line Therapy ™ developed by Tad James is a hypnotherapeutic device enabling the tracking back through time (biological time (since you were conceived)) ancestral time (within the scope of your genealogy) or past lives (we can all trace back to original humans – thus we are all inter-related at some level, and the work sometimes takes the client out of obvious linear scales).

Say you have a horrific accident. In that traumatic moment your brain gets re-wired to prevent you getting into that situation ever again – so fears arise, sweating, rapid breathing, heart rate rises etc – all designed to get adrenalin flowing. The TimeLine takes you back to just before the original accident and enables the client to soak up a feeling of life without that extra stress factor. Returning to the here and now induces an ability to challenge triggers more successfully and leave behind aspects that no longer serve you.

Constellation Therapy

Constellation was a development of gestalt therapy where aspects of psychology are broken down into constituent parts, examined and then put back together to create a slightly (or greatly) altered image. The principle that underlies constellations is that there is a field of hidden dynamics that each of us carries whether we are aware of it and whether we have access to the information that would either prove or disprove that knowledge. By using some form of representation in the form of people in a workshop, or playpeople, or pieces of felt, those hidden dynamics can therefore be observed, and some healing dialogue can be enabled.

So how can a constellation help build resilience. The principle here is that inherited trauma is a real thing – study scientifically:

Researchers in California published a study of Civil War prisoners that came to a remarkable conclusion. Male children of abused war prisoners were about 10 percent more likely to die than their peers were in any given year after middle age, the study reported.

The findings, the authors concluded, supported an "epigenetic explanation." The idea is that trauma can leave a chemical mark on a person's genes, which then is passed down to subsequent generations. The mark doesn't directly damage the gene; there's no mutation. Instead it alters the mechanism by which the gene is converted into functioning proteins or expressed. The alteration isn't genetic. It's epigenetic.

The field of epigenetics gained momentum about a decade ago, when scientists reported that children who were exposed in the womb to the Dutch Hunger Winter, a period of famine toward the end of World War II, carried a particular chemical mark, or epigenetic signature, on one of their genes. The researchers later linked that finding to differences in the children's health later in life, including higher-than-average body mass.

The excitement since then has only intensified, generating more studies — of the descendants of Holocaust survivors, of victims of poverty — that hint at the heritability of trauma. If these studies hold up, they would suggest that we inherit some trace of our parents' and even grandparents' experience, particularly their suffering, which in turn modifies our own day-to-day health — and perhaps our children's, too.

In view of this fact, which has now been shown proof of, the work of the constellation enables the confining of historic issues to history. In the case of say, the descendent of a capo employed at Auschwitz who was murdered before reconciling with any of the guilt he might have had or perhaps not had prior to his eventual murder by the Nazis. The fact that he was a capo might place a shame within the family system of such proportion that the subject and his name are never ever mentioned.

In the context of a constellation, the responsibility for the choices that were made can be shown to ONLY belong to the ancestor capo, and hence the descendent has completely relinquished the hold on that shame. In that moment the shame disappears from the current system and the person undertaking the constellation walks away more resilient and clear of the old shame and may find themselves able to talk about the subject without any problem. The example given was an actual piece of work I conducted in 2011, and to my knowledge the nightmares that had plagued the client stopped and have not returned. Frequent nightmares can easily be shown to induce stress and reduce quality of life. The knock-on effect of that could easily be some chronic health issue such as depression.

Meditation

To help build resilience in later life, review early childhood and allow your mind to wander – was there a teacher, a neighbour or a relative who just seemed to "get" you without the need of a long diatribe to facilitate understanding. Start by thanking them for their support and begin in a mild meditative state to explore that relationship. The state I am referring to here is similar to when you have been sitting in front of the TV for 40 minutes but have no idea what you are watching despite not actually being asleep.

In those wanderings of mind allow your cell memory to reveal things that seem to relate but acknowledge that as they come up you have no idea how they fit in, until you do know!

Also in your meditations go to a place that always felt safe, and if that eludes you, create one in such a journey – a beach, a wood, a meadow – these natural places often (but not always) have that peace and tranquillity to enable you to feel safe.

Shamanic Journey work

In shamanic journey work, you will allow your imagination to scour the histories in your conscious mind, and the archives of your cell memory and sub-conscious mind to explore an unlikely world. However, the purpose is to enable you to relinquish trauma, and perhaps to have a conversation with some relative that perhaps abused you, but who is now dead. That conversation is of course unlikely in the real world, but can have tremendous value in the subconscious, because it enables the survivor to get power over the traumas and things that happened that shouldn't have happened, or the things that didn't happen but that should have happened in a supportive childhood. Allowing animistic elements to enter that field enables safe support that can later be accessed at any time and builds on the resilience that you have found.

Combinations of therapies

I highly recommend combinations provide the boundaries to each type of work is observed and understood by both client and the practitioner. Otherwise the capacity to get lost is quite high!

When you take a car to a garage for repair, the engineer will have a large toolbox and will carefully select the right tool for the job. It is the same with therapeutic work.

Building Resilience

Appendices

ACEs Scoring Sheet

Prior to your 18th birthday:

1. Did a parent or other adult in the household often or very often... Swear at you, insult you, put you down, or humiliate you? or Act in a way that made you afraid that you might be physically hurt?
   No___If Yes, enter 1 ___
2. Did a parent or other adult in the household often or very often... Push, grab, slap, or throw something at you? or Ever hit you so hard that you had marks or were injured?
   No___If Yes, enter 1 ___
3. Did an adult or person at least 5 years older than you ever... Touch or fondle you or have you touch their body in a sexual way? or Attempt or actually have oral, anal, or vaginal intercourse with you?
   No___If Yes, enter 1 ___
4. Did you often or very often feel that ... No one in your family loved you or thought you were important or special? or Your family didn't look out for each other, feel close to each other, or support each other?
   No___If Yes, enter 1 ___
5. Did you often or very often feel that ... You didn't have enough to eat, had to wear dirty clothes, and had no one to protect you? or Your parents were too drunk or high to take care of you or take you to the doctor if you needed it?
   No___If Yes, enter 1 __
6. Were your parents ever separated or divorced?
   No___If Yes, enter 1 ___
7. Was your mother or stepmother:
   Often or very often pushed, grabbed, slapped, or had

[31]

something thrown at her? or Sometimes, often, or very often kicked, bitten, hit with a fist, or hit with something hard? or Ever repeatedly hit over at least a few minutes or threatened with a gun or knife?
No___If Yes, enter 1 ___

8. Did you live with anyone who was a problem drinker or alcoholic, or who used street drugs?
No___If Yes, enter 1 ___

9. Was a household member depressed or mentally ill, or did a household member attempt suicide?   No___If Yes, enter 1 ___

10. Did a household member go to prison?
No___If Yes, enter 1 ___

Bibliography

Hamish Edgar - Limbic Reflexology: Student Textbook Revised Edition

Nadine Burke Harris – Deepest Well

Julia Buckley – Heal Me

Rafe Nauen - Family Constellations – Unravelling the Mystery of your ancestral Timeline

Stephan Hausner – Even if it costs me my life

Nadine Burke Harris - The Deepest Well

John Bradshaw - Healing the shame that binds us

Websites

https://acestoohigh.com/got-your-ace-score/

https://www.ncbi.nlm.nih.gov/pmc/articles/PMC3679131/

https://www.ted.com/talks/nadine_burke_harris_how_childhood_trauma_affects_health_across_a_lifetime

http://whatisepigenetics.com

http://www.lotusholistic.com

http://limbicreflexology.co.uk

http://neuroplastix.com/

https://rafenauen.com

https://rafesworkshops.com

http://building-resilience.co.uk

https://www.acesconnection.com

About the Author

Rafe Nauen was born in 1950 in Orpington Kent. He is married to Julie Bowman and has 8 children and 14 grandchildren. He works in Derby as an EFT, NLP and constellation practitioner to private and business customers. The workshops and one to one sessions are places where people can find out quite a bit more about who they really are.

Printed in Great Britain
by Amazon